MW01470137

Reliquary Of English Song

RELIQUARY OF ENGLISH SONG

FIFTY-TWO EARLY ENGLISH SONGS FROM CIRCA 1250 TO 1700

COLLECTED AND EDITED, WITH AN HISTORICAL
INTRODUCTION AND NOTES

BY

FRANK HUNTER POTTER

THE ACCOMPANIMENTS HARMONIZED AND ARRANGED BY

CHARLES VINCENT, Mus. Doc. Oxon.

AND

T. TERTIUS NOBLE, Mus. Doc. Oxon.

Price, $1.25 *net*

G. SCHIRMER

NEW YORK
3 EAST 43D STREET

LONDON, W.
18, BERNERS STREET

RELIQUARY OF ENGLISH SONG

FIFTY-TWO EARLY ENGLISH SONGS FROM
CIRCA 1250 TO 1700

COLLECTED AND EDITED, WITH AN HISTORICAL
INTRODUCTION AND NOTES

BY

FRANK HUNTER POTTER

THE ACCOMPANIMENTS HARMONIZED AND ARRANGED BY
CHARLES VINCENT, Mus. Doc. Oxon.

AND

T. TERTIUS NOBLE, Mus. Doc. Oxon.

Price, 1.25 *net*

G. SCHIRMER

NEW YORK
3 EAST 43D STREET

LONDON, W.
18, BERNERS STREET

MUSIC

Introduction

The English possess an heritage of song scarcely equalled by that of any other nation in Europe. Indeed, it may be said that up to the advent of the great *lieder*-writers of Germany during the last century the mass of English songs was both greater and more varied than any other. It had been enriched not only by the compositions of a race of musicians distinguished in secular music at a time when no other country could boast such a possession in similar numbers, but also by the contributions of the common people and the humbler minstrels in countless folk-songs, many of which are of the highest beauty.

As far back as we know anything, England was an intensely musical country. In the time of the Saxon Chroniclers the land was ringing with melody, and long before the middle of the thirteenth century there must have been a fixed school of English song, for it takes hundreds of years to produce a national type, and we know that one was in existence at that period. "Sumer is icumen in," dating from about A. D. 1250, is one of the oldest piece of secular music of any country which can now be read. It is thoroughly and entirely English in its quality, bearing no resemblance to the folk-music of any other land, but being of precisely the same character as a mass of bold, vigorous songs which we find in English folk-music four hundred years later. It was this vigorous, lusty quality which gave the country its name "Merrie England," for that was what "merrie" meant in its original sense.

Throughout early English literature the story is the same, from Piers Plowman down. Chaucer's Squire in the Canterbury Tales "went singing and fluting all the day," and nearly every other character on that wonderful pilgrimage had some contribution of music to make.

By the time of Henry VIII the preëminence of the English as a musical nation was recognized throughout Europe. Erasmus writes that "they excel the whole world in the beauty of their women, their knowledge of music and the excellence of their table." Similar testimony is given by the Venetian Ambassadors to Henry VIII. These were men of the ripest culture, some of them good musicians themselves, and their reports to the Venetian Republic, which are still preserved, speak of English music in the warmest terms. One of them says of the choristers of the royal chapel that "their voices were rather divine than human; they did not chant, but sang like angels."

In the reigns of Henry VIII and Elizabeth music was practised universally and held in the highest estimation by people of every rank. Not only was it a necessary qualification of ladies and gentlemen, but even the City of London advertised the musical abilities of boys educated in Bridewell or Christ's Hospital as a mode of recommending them as servants or apprentices. Lutes hung in every hall, while virginal, cittern and viol, for the amusement of waiting customers, were as necessary a part of the furniture of barber-shops as are newspapers to-day.

This universal practice of music continued. A hundred years after Elizabeth's time Pepys, who gives such a graphic picture of contemporary manners, shows on what a musical basis his own household was organized. He had a boy to wait on himself and a maid for his wife. Four maids are mentioned in the Diary. The first sang, the second played the "harpsichon," and he bought a Virginal book for her. The third also played, and the fourth sang, while the boy both played the lute and sang. In this way Pepys had the materials for a concert in his own house, and the Diary is evidence of how much he employed them.

Henry VIII was very musical. He sang and played the lute and virginals, and there are several songs of his composition. He had distinguished musicians about him, like Byrd and Tallis and Gibbons, but they are mostly remembered by their church compositions. This reign is marked by one unfortunate event, the destruction of the old ballads. During the throes of the Reformation these ballads were often put to partisan uses, and a general destruction of them was ordered by Henry. Because of this, and of their naturally frail character, there exist almost no black-letter ballads older than this reign.

The reign of Elizabeth was peculiarly rich in music, as it was in poetry. Indeed, the Renaissance seems to have affected music as much in England as it did in Italy, but along perfectly individual lines. The art-songs of the period, as contradistinguished from the popular ballads, received their character in a measure from the contrapuntal compositions, madrigals and the like, which were the serious concern of the musicians of that time. These compositions had little or no melody in the modern sense of the word, as a general thing, and the songs which resembled them were often stiff and formal, though as a class they hardly deserved the characterization of an irate critic who said that they were "as misshapen as if they had been composed of notes scattered about by chance, instead of being cast in a regular mould."

Even in these art-songs the melodic instinct asserted itself occasionally and produced tuneful melodies like Morley's "It was a lover and his lass," or Dowland's "Now, O now," which even obtained the distinction of being adopted as popular ballads, and were commonly sung about England as late as the middle of the last century. In fact, two streams of music were running side by side, the art-form and the popular ballad, and the former was being gradually modified by the latter. The same thing was going on in Italy, where popular airs, sometimes even of scandalous origin, were being adapted to sacred music.

Another powerful influence on the character of English song should be remembered. There always existed, even in compositions of the popular sort, a disposition to fit the music closely to the poetry, sometimes even to particular words. An example of this is to be found in the old ballad, "Ah! the syghes that come fro' my heart," where an attempt is made to give pathos to the words "from my love depart," which reminds one, in intent at least, of the efforts of the whole modern school.

This was also the declared object of certain early Italian composers, but in Italy it vanished from the opera aria, which became the prevailing form, while in England it effected a permanent lodgment in the song, which was there the national form, just as the aria was in Italy.

Perhaps the foremost exponent of this fitting of sound to sense was Henry Lawes, who flourished during the reigns of James I and Charles I, dying after the Restoration. Owing to this quality, all the foremost poets of his time, from Milton and Waller downwards, gave him their verses to set. Lawes wished to "set words with just note and accent," and the praise of Milton and Waller, which is quoted in another place in this volume, testifies to how well he succeeded, in the estimation of his contemporaries. On the other hand, as a taste for Italian music grew in England, Lawes became neglected, and such critics as Hawkins and Burney, a century after his death, could find no good in him at all. But as his airs are often charming and always appropriate and expressive, they are beginning to come into their own again after two centuries.

Music was by no means so completely banished from England during the Commonwealth as is commonly believed. Of course the King's band was dispersed, and the cathedral and church services were discontinued, but there was plenty of music in private.

24814

Both Cromwell and Milton were devotedly fond of it, and the careers of two musicians who are represented by songs in this collection disprove the idea that it was officially prohibited. Henry Lawes, who did not follow his brother William into the Royalist army, supported himself by giving singing lessons and published several volumes of songs during this period, while Dr. John Wilson, who as a boy had sung in Shakespeare's plays, was appointed Professor of Music at Oxford about the time Lawes published his songs.

The Restoration was followed by a revival of secular music which was influenced to some extent by the personal preferences of Charles II, who had contracted a taste for French music during his residence abroad. But this had no permanent effect; the national spirit was too strong, and besides, the succeeding reigns were marked by the career of the greatest and most original musical genius whom England has ever produced, Henry Purcell. He worked in every field, religious, dramatic, lyric and instrumental, and in every one of them he did something new, and exerted a lasting influence. Many of his vocal compositions are so overladen with ornament, after the fashion of his day, that they are not available for modern use, but occasionally he produced a piece of flowing melody of surpassing beauty, and in his operas scenes of splendid dramatic force. It has been claimed for him that he was the originator of English melody, but this is hardly true. The Pastoral, that one of his forms which has persisted most strongly in English song, and which is generally accepted as being most characteristically English, was in existence as far back as we know anything.

The two streams of song above mentioned, the art-song and the popular ballad, continued to flow side by side, influencing one another more and more, till they may be said to have fairly come together in the person of Thomas Augustine Arne, whose graceful, flowing melodies unite the distinction of the older song-writers to the undeniable charm of the English ballad. From Arne's time for three quarters of a century the English song reached its greatest popularity, and was produced in incredible numbers.

There were several reasons for this. In the first place, "serious" opera, that is, opera with recitatives in place of spoken dialogue, never took root in England. Almost the only example of it which had any lasting popularity was Arne's "Artaxerxes," which held the public favor for nearly three quarters of a century. The really popular English opera was in what is known as the "opéra comique" form, that is, with the usual solos, concerted numbers and ensembles, connected by spoken dialogue. All the works of this kind were akin to the famous "Beggar's Opera," which was said to have made "Rich gay and Gay rich," in allusion to the names of the manager and author. They were not necessarily ballad-operas, as that was, made up of verses set to old ballad-tunes; they had the usual assortment of songs and concerted pieces, and they often included numbers from Italian and other sources which were frankly acknowledged, by the way. Nothing more was asked of the composer who put together a piece than that he should produce an agreeable entertainment, and no fault was found with him, especially towards the end of the eighteenth century, if he introduced selections by Italians, Frenchmen or Germans. He usually wrote the overture, the finales and a considerable proportion of the solos and concerted pieces, and in this way the supply of English songs was continually growing.

Another thing which contributed largely to this supply was that popular form of amusement, the concert-garden. All readers of English memoirs and fiction must remember the constant allusions to Ranelagh, Vauxhall and Marylebone. These gardens resembled those in a modern German or French watering-place. They had orchestras and organs, and they engaged the most popular singers of the day. They had, too,

24814

composers retained on permanent salaries to supply these singers with new songs, and the first musicians of their time, Arne and Bishop, for instance, were not ashamed to hold these positions. As a consequence, the number of songs composed in this way was enormous; one man alone is known to have written over two thousand compositions for these gardens. Naturally, the vast majority of such songs, turned out mechanically, like chairs and tables from a furniture factory, had a strong family likeness and were thoroughly commonplace, but there were still among them many of great beauty and real inspiration.

A third cause which tended to foster the production of English songs in the old style was that extreme conservatism of a large section of the English public, which was so well expressed in the character of Squire Western in "Tom Jones." The spirit which would hear nothing but good old English tunes naturally helped the creation of others of similar character, and that robust patriotism which despised everything foreign long kept undefiled the spring of English melody.

With the end of the eighteenth century the English song begins to decline. The introduction of foreign airs in the operas of Storace and Kelly, among others, had its effect on the one hand, while another group turned to the older ballad-forms for their inspiration. Moreover, there were fewer distinguished song-writers. Bishop had talent, but was overworked and careless, while Balfe and Wallace were getting away from the old forms. Sterndale Bennett wrote some exquisite songs, but they were few, and with him the classical period may be said to have ended.

In the following volumes an especial effort has been made to give the words and music of the songs in their original form. This has not always been possible, for the taste of the seventeenth and eighteenth centuries was not that of to-day, and our ancestors enjoyed a vulgarity which now would disgust. Consequently, it has sometimes been necessary to alter the lyrics or substitute others. Except in these cases, it is believed that complete fidelity to the original texts has been preserved.

The editor wishes to express his indebtedness to the monumental works of Chappell, Baring-Gould and Hatton. No collection of English songs can be made to-day without reference to them. And he wishes to acknowledge an especial obligation to Mr. Edmonstoune Duncan, one of the foremost authorities on English song, who has been good enough to make a number of suggestions which have been incorporated in the following notes.

F. H. P.

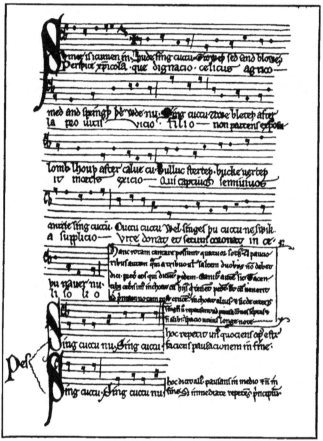

Sumer is icumen in.

Notes

Mr. Duncan calls attention to the interesting fact that the Norsemen founded kingdoms in England, Scotland, Ireland, France and Spain, so that their minstrels, the Scalds, were in a sense behind the music of these nations. Unfortunately, not a note of their compositions survives, so that how large an influence they had in moulding the songs of these nations must remain a matter of speculation. It is a fact, however, that certain songs are common to several of these countries, both as to words and music. Dr. Crotch pointed out that Welsh and Danish airs have a close kinship, and Engel tells us that the air "Ar hyd y nos," still popular in Wales, is also current in Jutland. This, however, cannot be taken as proving too much, for many songs have been carried from one country to another in relatively recent times, and have attained wide popularity. Such a case is "What if a day, or a month, or a year," referred to later in these notes.

It was a characteristic of the Norsemen that they should in a short space of time lose their racial traits and assume those of the people among whom they had settled. So they became Frenchmen in Normandy, Spaniards in Spain and Italians in Sicily and Naples. Therefore the Norse type, whatever it may have been, probably did not long persist, and when we reach our first song, the English type is firmly fixed.

Sumer is   THIS song, which is among the Harleian manuscripts in the British Museum,
icumen in.   has been the subject of some controversy as to its period, but it is now generally accepted as being of the thirteenth century, a date which is assigned to it by the distinguished antiquarian Ritson. The facsimile shows it to be, if sung as originally intended, a six-part round, so constructed that four equal voices should sing the melody in canon, while two add a drone bass. Chappell asserts that the instrument on which a tune was composed was infallibly revealed by the character of the music. If this be true, this smooth, flowing melody would seem to point to the fiddle as its originator, for it is quite distinct from the bold, somewhat abrupt character which marks harp music, or the jerky quality which marks the bagpipe's tunes. These three were the instruments in common use in England at the time the song was written. As has been said, this is one of the earliest secular songs which can now be deciphered.

Ah! the syghes that   THE unfortunate destruction of the ballads, which has been referred to
come fro' my heart.   in the introduction, is probably one of the reasons why we have no songs which can be assigned with certainty to any period before the reign of Henry VIII. There are many which are undoubtedly of much greater antiquity, for popular songs are long-lived, as will be seen by many examples to which reference will be made, but they often afford no internal evidence as to their age. "Ah! the syghes that come fro' my heart" is at any rate at least as old as the time of Henry VII. The little cadence or flourish is characteristic of the period, and is found also in the next song, while the pretty attempt at musical expression on the words "from my love depart" is the earliest known example of what was to be a leading characteristic of English song, and which is referred to in the introduction.

Pastime with   THE words and music of this song are preserved in a manuscript of the time of
good company.   Henry VIII in the British museum, in which it is called "The King's Ballad." Henry, who was a younger son, and succeeded to the position of Heir Apparent only on the death of his elder brother, Arthur, was originally designed for the church. He was consequently instructed in music, which was then a requirement of an ecclesiastic, and he is known to have written two masses, a motet, an anthem, some songs and various other compositions, vocal and instrumental. There is no doubt of the authenticity of "Pastime with good company," and it gained great popularity, being found or referred to in a number of early publications.

The Hunt is up.   AMONG the favorites of Henry VIII, says Chappell, Puttenham notices
     "one Gray, what good estimation did he grow into with the same King Henry, and afterwards with the Duke of Somerset, Protector, for making certain merry ballads, whereof one chiefly was 'The hunte is up, the hunte is up'."

It is not certain, though it is considered highly probable, that the tune here given is the one above mentioned, for any song intended to arouse a sleeper in the morning, even a love-song, was called a "Hunt's up," the term being equivalent to the French word *aubade*. And this tune itself is found in various versions.

You Gentlemen of England. THE ballad now known as "You Gentlemen of England" is an alteration of one by Martin Parker, a copy of which is in the Pepys Collection. It is in black letter and entitled "Saylers for my money; a new ditty composed in the praise of saylers and sea affayres; briefly shewing the nature of so worthy a calling and the effects of their industry; to the tune of The Jovial Cobbler." Instead of "You Gentlemen of England" it begins, "Countriemen of England."

Martin Parker lived in the reign of Charles I, so that the words are much more modern than the tune, which dates back to the time of Henry VIII or earlier. It was these words, however, which gained the song its popularity, for the old words seem irretrievably lost and the tune has always been referred to as "You Gentlemen of England," ever since Parker's words appeared. It is one of the lastingly popular sea-songs of England.

All attempts to find the original words of The Jovial Cobbler have failed, but the tune is believed to be as old as the reign of Elizabeth. There is another ballad, "The Jovial Cobbler of St. Helen's," but it has quite a different meter. There are various versions of "You Gentlemen of England" in Ritson, with some fifteen different verses, from which those in the text are selected.

The Three Ravens. THIS is one of those songs which are undoubtedly much older than the period when they are first printed. Its earliest appearance in print, so far as we know, was in 1611, in "Country Pastimes," but it is much more archaic than the music of that period. Whether this is one of the songs which is a common heritage from the Scalds is of course uncertain, but Mr. Duncan says that there is a Danish version of it, as well as the comparatively well-known Scottish one, "The Twa Corbies."

I live not where I love. FEW English ballads have exceeded this one in popularity. There are many versions of it, and it is known all over England. I myself, when on a visit there, have heard a version of it sung by an inmate of the "Union," as the English call their poor-houses, in Lymington, Hampshire, which shows how lasting this popularity is. The tune was hardly recognizable at first, for the singer was very old, and the words were greatly changed, but there could be no question about the identity of the song.

Such changes in words and music are common, and one of the most amusing examples of them is the version of this very song which Hazlitt used to sing to Douglas Jerrold and his friends. Jerrold was delighted with the relation between cause and effect in the following stanza, which is an admirable example of the way ballads come to vary and deteriorate in the mouths of ignorant singers, and which is especially common with English or Scotch or Irish ballads which have been brought over to America.

> If all the world was of one religion,
> Many a living thing would die
> Before that I would forget my true love
> Or in any way his love deny;
> My heart should change and be more strange,
> If ever I'd inconstant prove;
> My heart is with him altogether,
> Though I live not where I love.

The words in the text are from Chappell's edition of the Roxburghe Ballads.

Thomas Morley. THE next two songs, "It was a lover and his lass" and "Now is the month of maying" are of peculiarly English types. The first, which is in "As You Like It," is an admirable example of the smooth, flowing pastoral which was represented by the very first song of our collection, and which will be found to persist through the whole course of English music. It is, moreover, one of the very few of the airs which were sung in the original productions of Shakespeare's plays which are now known, and of this small number two at least were written by Morley. The second air, "Now is the month of maying," is a notable example of the Fa-la or Ballet, a form of composition for several voices, very popular at this period, and of which Morley was a first-rate master.

24814

Thomas Morley, the composer of these songs, was born in 1557, was a Gentleman of the Chapel Royal, and became organist of St. Paul's in 1591. He died in 1603, after a life which seems to have been uneventful except for a period about 1591, when he appears to have been a "promoter," or spy engaged in betraying Catholics. He composed many songs, madrigals, anthems and services which are still extant.

O Willow, Willow. DESDEMONA'S song in "Othello" is one of the best known of the traditional Shakespeare airs. It is found in various publications and in differing versions. Shakespeare's is given in our text; another is found in a little manuscript volume in the British Museum, where it faces "Have you seen but a white lily grow." We reproduce both songs in our illustrations.

The ballad was quite proverbial, for it was parodied (and that is a complete test of currency) so late as 1686, in the reign of James II, when it appears in Playford's Pleasant Musical Companion as "A poor soul sat sighing by a gingerbread stall." This is an unusual period for a song to remain popular in the metropolis. Others have far outlived this span, but generally in remote parts of the country, not in London.

Among the varying versions that in the British Museum manuscript, which is assigned to the early part of the seventeenth century by experts, is one of the most interesting. It is worth while to compare it with the Shakespeare version, so we give it here. It will be seen that Shakespeare has somewhat varied his, to fit a female character.

> A poor soul sat sighing by a sycamore tree
> With his hand in his bosom and his head upon his knee.
> O willow, willow, willow, must be my garland.
>
> He sighed in his singing and made a great moan,
> I am dead to all pleasure, my true love she is gone.
> O willow, etc.
>
> The mute bird sat by him was made tame by his moans,
> The true tears fell from him would have melted the stones.
> O willow, etc.
>
> Come all you forsaken and mourn you with me,
> Who speaks of a false love, mine's falser than she.
> O willow, etc.
>
> Let love no more boast in her palace nor bower,
> It buds, but it blasteth ere it be a flower.
> O willow, etc.
>
> Though fair and more false I die with thy wound,
> Thou hast lost the truest lover that goes upon the ground.
> O willow, etc.
>
> Let nobody chide her, her scorns I approve.
> She was born to be false and I to die for her love.
> O willow, etc.
>
> Take this for my farewell and latest adieu,
> Write this on my tomb, in love I was true.
> O willow, etc.

It will be observed that the accompaniment in the reproductions both of this song and of "Have you seen but a white lily grow" are in an unusual notation. This is what is known as lute tablature, a form of notation employed for lutes and other stringed instruments of the same character. The lines represent the six principal strings of the instrument; the letters on those lines indicate the frets by which the strings are shortened, as with a guitar; and the little marks above the letters, somewhat like the tails of our eighth- and sixteenth-notes, show the duration of the note.

The lute was a troublesome instrument in many ways. The tremendous strain on the belly was always racking it to pieces, so that continual repairs were necessary, and a lute-player who lived in Paris remarked that in that city it cost about the same to keep a horse or a lute. It was also difficult to keep in tune, and another famous musician calculated that in the life of any lute-player eighty years old, sixty years at least had been passed in tuning his instrument.

The British
Grenadiers. THE date of this tune is uncertain, but it is clearly much older than the words, and from its likeness to two other airs, whose date is known, namely, "Sir Edward Noel's delight" and "All you that are good fellows," it has been assigned to the same period, the reign of Elizabeth. The date of the words is equally uncertain, but it cannot be earlier than 1678, when the grenadier company was formed, nor later than the reign of Queen Anne, when the grenadiers ceased to carry hand-grenades.

Love will find
out the way. THIS tune is another which has had a lasting popularity in England, for while it has been printed in numerous collections ever since it appeared in Playford's "Musicks Recreations on the Lyra Viol," it was so recently as 1860 taken down by a Kentish organist from the lips of a hop-picker. The words used here are in Percy's "Reliques"; other versions are found in several other collections, differing widely among themselves.

What if a day. THERE are few English songs which afford more room for speculation than this one. Its origin and its authorship are both in doubt, for it is one of those songs which are found in two countries, and while it has been ascribed to a particular author, there is presumptive evidence that it was popular long before he was born.

"What if a day" is well known in Holland under the title of "Berg op Zoom," in which shape it will be found in Kremser's "Altniederländische Volkslieder." Here it is a patriotic song of splendid martial vigor. But it is also found in a Dutch publication of 1647 under the name of "Essex's Lamentation." Furthermore, Herr Daniel de Lange, a distinguished Dutch musician and Director of the Amsterdam Conservatory of Music, informed the writer that Holland had few if any original folk-songs; that most of those current there could be traced back to an English, French or German origin. From these facts, it would seem probable that the tune is English and was carried over to Holland by some of Elizabeth's soldiers who fought in the Low Countries.

There is some doubt as to the authorship. In one or two early collections it is assigned to Thomas Campion, but that means nothing, for editors were flagrantly careless about such things at that period and much later. Playford was the most careful of them, yet the song "Why should'st thou swear" was assigned to no less than three different composers in three successive editions of his "Ayres," all published within seven years. Neither words nor music of "What if a day" are to be found in the collection of Campion's songs, and from the dates of references to it and the similarity of its words to older songs, it may very well belong to a much earlier period than the beginning of the seventeenth century, when Campion lived.

Have you seen but
a white lily grow. THIS delightful little song, by an unknown composer, is found face to face with "O Willow, Willow," in a little manuscript book in the British Museum. This book, to which reference has already been made in the paragraph about the Willow song, is numbered Add. Ms. fol. 15117, fol. 17b.

It will also be observed in the illustrations that the writing of the words of one song is quite different from that of the other. That of "O Willow" is said by experts to be much the older, as might be expected from the character of the tunes, and that these songs of different dates are in the same volume need excite no surprise, for songs were often inserted in a manuscript volume long after it was originally made, wherever there was an empty page.

John Dowland. THE composer of the next three songs had a more adventurous career than fell to the lot of most musicians of his time. The date of his birth is not known, but before he was twenty years of age he was in the service of Sir Edward Cobham, English Ambassador at Paris, where he was converted to Catholicism. On his return to England he applied for a position in the service of Queen Elizabeth, but failed. "My religion was my hindrance," he says, "whereupon my mind being troubled I desired to get beyond the seas." He entered the service of the Duke of Brunswick, Landgrave of Hesse, and afterwards went to Venice and Florence. He intended going to Rome, but at Florence he fell in with a number of English recusants, and frightened by being with men who were plotting treason against Elizabeth, he refused offers of service with the Pope and several cardinals, and went back to Nuremberg.

24814

Haue yo[u] seene but a Whyte Lillie grow before Rude hands had tucht it, haue yo[u]

markt but the fall of the Snow before the Earthe hathe Smucht it, haue yo[u] felt the w...

wooll of Beuer, or Swans downe Euer, or haue smelt of the Bud of the Bryer, or the Nard in the

fire or haue tasted the bagge of the Bee, o so whyte, o so soft o so sweet, so sweete is Shee.

In 1598 he was appointed lutenist to Christian IV of Denmark, returning to London in 1606. He was appointed one of the King's musicians of the lutes in 1612, and died in 1625.

Dowland published various volumes of songs, as well as lessons and pieces for the lute. Not only is the music of his songs good, but the lyrics, which were written by himself, were of such beauty that they have been included, without the music, in various collections of poetry. He was held in high esteem by his contemporaries, and Shakespeare, in that one of his sonnets in "The Passionate Pilgrim" beginning "If music and sweet poetry agree," refers to him thus:

> "Dowland to thee is dear, whose heavenly touch
> Upon the lute doth ravish human sense."

Of the three songs in this collection, "Now, O now" has acquired the greatest popularity, being still heard as a folk-song in various parts of England.

Once I loved a maiden fair. THIS little ballad is an example of the Laments which constitute so important an element in English songs; another example will be found later in "Barbara Allen." Their simple pathos appealed so strongly to the people that they were produced in great numbers, just as were the rhymed confessions and last speeches of criminals who had been executed.

The ballad as printed in the Roxburghe Collection contains twelve verses, from which these three have been selected.

Tobacco's but an Indian weed. THIS song is contained in a manuscript of the reign of James I, himself a bitter hater of the weed, and author of the famous tract, "A Counterblaste to Tobacco." George Withers, who wrote the words, was a "Presbyterian satirist," according to Wood, and may well have written this song to show his contempt for the King.

However that may be, it secured great popularity on its own merits. Its symbolic character appealed strongly to the mass of people, and though it originally figured as a comic song in the "Merry Drollery" collection of 1670 and in Tom Durfey's "Wit and Mirth" of 1690, it soon came into use as a hymn, being adapted by Ralph Erskine as a gospel sonnet under the title of "Smoking Spiritualized." No less a person than Samuel Wesley reset the words of the original poem to music of his own, but the old air kept its place. It is still in use, and Dr. Vincent says that he himself has heard it sung in Dissenting chapels in England.

Phillida and Coridon. THIS graceful song is found in "Pills to Purge Melancholy," but is probably much older than the date of that work. Neither author nor composer is known.

Wronge not, deare empress. NOTHING is known of this song, except that it was found in a manuscript (D 3850) in the Drexel Collection in the New York Public Library, where it was unearthed by the writer. From the character of the writing and the style of the air it would appear to belong to the early part of the reign of Charles I, though there is no clue to either author or composer.

Why should'st thou sweare. THOUGH this air is set down in the first edition of Playford's "Select Musical Ayres" as a "French Ayre," while in the second edition is it assigned to "Mr. Charles" and in the third to Henry Lawes, there is reason to accept the musical tradition which recognizes King Charles the First as the composer. In the second edition, where it is ascribed to "Mr. Charles," it is printed along with a group of songs by Nicholas Laneare, who has lent his name to conceal his master's in other collections. It might well be that the identity of the composer was concealed in the first edition for political reasons, half revealed in the second, and again concealed in the third for the same reasons, or the variations in the assignments may have come from sheer carelessness, as was so often the case with musical publications of this period. At any rate, there is no difficulty in accepting the tradition, for Charles was an excellent musician, a pupil of Coperario (John Cooper was his name), who was the teacher of Henry and William Lawes, and of many other distinguished musicians of the period. Charles both played and composed, and there are a few other songs known to be by him, though he never proclaimed himself their author, as was the the wont of Henry VIII.

Phillis, on the
new-made hay.

THIS tune, another excellent example of the pastoral, is from "Pills to Purge Melancholy," but it has been necessary to change the words.

Sally in our Alley.

HENRY CAREY, the author of the words of this song, but not of the tune, was a well-known composer of the eighteenth century, and one of the men to whom the authorship of "God Save the King" has been assigned. "Sally in our Alley," of which he wrote both the words and the original tune, now discarded, attained a rapid popularity which has lasted in England to the present day. Carey gives the following account of its genesis:

"A vulgar error having prevailed among many persons, who imagine Sally Salisbury the subject of this ballad, the author begs to undeceive and assure them that it has not the least allusion to her, he being a stranger to her very name at the time this ballad was composed. For as innocence and virtue were ever the boundaries of his muse, so in this little poem he had no other view than to set forth the beauty of a chaste and disinterested passion, even in the lowest class of human life. The real occasion was this: a shoemaker's apprentice making holiday with his sweetheart, treated her with a sight of Bedlam, the puppet shows, the flying chairs and all the elegancies of Moorfields, from whence proceeding to the farthing-pye-house, he gave her a collation of buns, cheesecakes, gammon of bacon, stuffed beef and bottled ale, through all which scenes the author dodged them. Charmed by the simplicity of their courtship, he drew from what he had witnessed this little sketch of nature; but being then young and obscure, he was very much ridiculed by some of his acquaintance for this performance, which nevertheless made its way into the polite world, and amply recompensed him by the applause of the Divine Addison, who was pleased more than once to mention it with approbation." .

The touch of nature in the words has secured their continued popularity, but for the last hundred and fifty years they have been sung to the tune of "The Country Lass," which dates back to 1620 or earlier, Carey's tune having been quite forgotten.

Henry Lawes.

UNQUESTIONABLY the foremost name among the song-writers of the reign of Charles I was that of Henry Lawes. Not only was he admired by musicians, but his music was so well fitted to the words that the poets of the time vied with each other for the honor of having their verses set by him. His songs form an important part, perhaps the most important part, of the collections of the time.

He was the son of Thomas Lawes, a vicar-choral of Salisbury Cathedral, and was born at Dinton in Wiltshire, probably in December, 1595, as he was baptized on January 1st, 1596. He received his musical education from the John Cooper already referred to (Coperario), who taught music to the children of James I. Nothing seems to be known of his life until he was sworn in as Epistler to the Chapel Royal on January 1st, 1625-6, as Gentleman on November 3rd following, and soon afterwards as Clerk of the Cheque.

The first of his works which attracted general attention was his setting to music of Milton's "Comus." He was music-teacher in the family of the Earl of Bridgewater, and when that nobleman proposed giving a masque at Ludlow Castle, it was Lawes who suggested the choice of Milton to write it.

On the breaking out of the Rebellion, Henry did not follow his brother William into the Royalist army. Perhaps he was at heart inclined toward the Parliamentary side, for his suggestion of Milton to write Comus would seem to indicate an acquaintance, if not an intimacy, with that arch-traitor, as the Royalists regarded him. At any rate, after the suppression of the Chapel Royal and the King's private band, of which he was a member, he supported himself by giving singing lessons and by publishing certain volumes of songs. He probably took no side in politics, one way or the other, for he recovered his position in the Chapel Royal upon the Restoration, and composed the anthem, "Zadok the Priest," which was sung at the coronation of Charles II. He died in 1662, and was buried in the cloisters of Westminster Abbey.

Lawes composed the music for three masques, for two collections of psalms (one of them jointly with his brother William), and a great quantity of songs and dialogues for one or more voices, published in a number of collections, notably Playford's various editions of ' Musical Ayres." He held high rank in the esteem of his contemporaries, but soon lost credit. Hawkins declared that

HENRY LAWES Servant to his late Ma.ᵗⁱᵉ
in his publick and private Musick.

W.ᵐ Faithorne fecit

"in the time of Lawes the music of the English had scarce any melody at all," and his airs "differ widely from those of Carissimi and Marc Antonio Cesti, who were the first that introduced into music that elegant succession of harmonic intervals which is understood by the term melody." Dr. Burney considered his songs "languid and insipid, and equally devoid of learning and genius." Mr. Duncan points out, so far as Burney is concerned, that the learned doctor is equally hard on the poets of this time. He says that "there were certainly none which merited the title in any language of Europe," but as this condemnation would shut out such rhymesters as Milton, Ben Jonson, Herrick, Lovelace, Carew, Suckling, Waller, Crowley, Campion and Dowland in England alone, the value of his criticism may be inferred. Still, within half a century of his death, Lawes was forgotten; to-day he is being rediscovered. The reason is not far to seek.

As has been said in the introduction, Lawes' object was "to set words with just note and accent," and to make the prosody of his text the principal concern. In this he was supremely successful, at any rate in the judgment of the poets whose verses he set. Milton addressed to him the sonnet which, as Mr. Duncan so well says, "Chrystallized Lawes' lasting merit into verse":

> Harry, whose tuneful and well-measured song
> First taught our English music how to span
> Words with just note and accent, not to scan
> With **Midas'** cars, committing short and long;
>
> *   *   *   *   *   *   *   *
>
> To after age thou shalt be writ the man
> That with smooth air could'st humour best our tongue;
> Thou honour'st Verse, and Verse must lend her wing
> To honour thee, the Priest of Phœbus' quire.

Waller was even more emphatic:

> For as a window, thick with paint,
> Lets in a light but dim and faint,
> So others with division hide
> The light of sense, the poet's pride.
> But you alone may truly boast
> That not a syllable is lost.
>
> *   *   *   *   *   *   *
>
> Let those who only warble long
> And gargle in their throats a song,
> Content themselves with UT, RE, MI,
> Let words and sense be set by thee.

Clearly, Hawkins and Burney think Italian melody the only melody, while Waller thinks it no melody at all, a discussion whose echoes reach to our own time. Lawes himself, in the preface to his "Ayres and Dialogues," intimated little less than a dislike of the Italian style. He insisted that the English had produced as good music as any in Europe, and to ridicule the prevailing admiration for everything foreign, prints a song which he wrote as a hoax. He took the titles of a number of Italian airs from an index, strung them together, and set them to music. He gave out that the resulting song, which of course made complete nonsense, had just come from Italy, and then saw the public receive it with delight as an Italian composition.

Henry Lawes' songs have no characteristic of the Italian music of the day; they are thoroughly English. Sometimes, it is true, in the desire to fit the music to the words, he loses rhythmic quality, but to modern ears that is no crime. On the other hand, the extreme expressiveness of his music, in spite of its archaic form, wins for it to-day more admiration than has been given it by any one since his contemporaries.

Of the songs in this collection, the first seven are from Playford's "Select Musical Ayres" of the edition of 1652. "Little love serves my turn" and "I prethee send me back my heart" are from the edition of 1653.

No notice of Lawes seems adequate without some reference to his publisher, John Playford, who, having no business rivals, had a practical monopoly of the trade during his lifetime. With perhaps twenty exceptions, he published all the music issued in England during his career.

The Playford family was connected with music for sixty years from 1650. "Honest John Playford," as he was called (born in 1623), was the founder of the house. Among the works

24814

published by him, "The Dancing Master," published in 1650, is almost if not quite the most valuable. It is a collection of popular ballads and other airs of the period and earlier, arranged for the violin, to be used for country dances, and has proved a perfect mine of old English melodies. He also wrote a hand-book on the theory of music, which was so concise and plain that it might serve as a model to-day. It passed through nineteen or twenty editions, and remained the standard text-book on the subject for nearly a century.

Henry Playford succeeded his father, and published at least one book of the first importance, Purcell's "Orpheus Britannicus."

William Lawes. WILLIAM LAWES, the younger brother of Henry, was born at Salisbury in 1582. He received his musical education from Coperario at the cost of the Earl of Hertford. He joined the choir of Chichester Cathedral, and in 1602 left it to become a Gentleman of the Chapel Royal. At the outbreak of the Rebellion he joined the Royalist army, where his general, Lord Gerrard, appointed him to the commissariat in order to keep him out of danger. But according to Hawkins "the activity of his spirit disdained that security which was intended for him, and at the siege of Chester he lost his life by a casual shot. The King was so affected by his loss that he wore a particular mourning for him."

He wrote much vocal and instrumental music, but though an excellent musician, never in his own time achieved the fame of his brother. "Gather ye rosebuds," however, has been sung in concerts from his day till ours.

Dr. John Wilson. THE composer of the next song, "Wert thou more fairer than thou art," has been identified with that Jack Wilson who, as a boy, sang in Shakespeare's plays. He was born in 1594, became a Gentleman of the Chapel Royal, and was created doctor of music in 1644. He was considered the finest lute-player of his time, and Anthony-à-Wood speaks of him as a great humorist, and "the greatest and most curious judge of music ever was." He became Professor of Music at Oxford in 1656.

He composed many songs and a number of larger works, among which was a curious production entitled "Psalterium Carolinum. The Devotions of his Sacred Majestie in his Solitudes and Sufferings, Rendred in Verse. Set to Musick for 3 Voices and an Organ, or Theorbo."

The words of "Wert thou more fairer than thou art" have attracted several composers besides Wilson, among them being Henry Lawes and William Webb. There is also a setting in a collection published in 1760, entitled "Orpheus Britannicus," like Purcell's famous volume, but containing songs sung at Vauxhall and Marylebone Gardens, "or any other polite places of public entertainment."

When the King enjoys his own again. MARTIN PARKER, whom we have already met as the author of the words of "You Gentlemen of England," was a famous ballad-writer in the reign of Charles I. He was devoted to the Royalist cause, and in "Vox Borealis" in 1641 he was described, with much scurrilous abuse, as "The Prelate's Poet." It was in 1643 that he wrote "When the King enjoys his own again," one of the great songs of the world. Dryden commends him as the best ballad-maker of his day—a day when the ballad was a powerful religious and political force; and this particular song Ritson considered the most famous and popular ever heard in England. Invented to support the declining interests of Charles I, it served afterwards, he says, "with more success to keep up the spirit of Cavaliers, and promote the restoration of his son, an event which it was used to celebrate all over the Kingdom. At the Revolution (of 1688) it of course became an adherent of the exiled family, whose cause it never deserted, and as a song (Lilliburlero) is said to have been the principal means of depriving King James of the crown, so this very air, upon two memorable occasions, was very near being equally instrumental in replacing it on the head of his son. It is believed to be a fact that nothing fed the enthusiasm of the Jacobites, down almost to the present reign (Victoria) in every corner of Great Britain, more than 'The King shall enjoy his own again.'"

The air, which is sometimes claimed as Welsh, is really of unknown origin. Booker, Pond Rivers, Swallow, Dade and Dove, whose names are mentioned in the ballad, were all astrologers or almanac-makers of the day, the two occupations being pretty much the same.

AYRES
AND
DIALOGUES,

For One, Two, and Three Voyces.

BY

HENRY LAWES Servant to his late Majestie
in his Publick and Private Musick.

The First Booke,

LONDON,
Printed by T. H. for *John Playford*, and are to be sold at his Shop, in the Inner
Temple, near the Church door, 1653.

Barbara Allen.

BOTH England and Scotland have a ballad entitled "Barbara Allen," but the metre shows that there can never be any similarity in the tunes. The English version has been popular for many years. Goldsmith, in his third essay, says of it: "The music of the finest singer is dissonance to what I felt when our old dairy maid sung me into tears with Johnny Armstrong's Last Good-night, or the Cruelty of Barbara Allen." There are a number of versions of the ballad; that given in the text is from Percy's "Reliques." The tune is from tradition, and is from Chappell's "Popular Music of the Olden Time."

The Self-Banished.

DR. JOHN BLOW, born in 1648, was one of the first set of Children of the Chapel Royal on its reëstablishment under Captain Cooke at the Restoration in 1660. He was extremely precocious, and at the age of fifteen set three anthems which were performed by the choir. In 1669 he was appointed organist of Westminster, but is said to have resigned or been dismissed in 1680 to make room for Henry Purcell, on whose death in 1695 he was reappointed, and remained for the rest of his life. Blow's reputation as a composer was overshadowed by that of his great pupil, Purcell, but he had real originality. He composed much sacred music and a number of songs, glees, and catches. The words of "The Self-Banished" are by Edwin Walm, and the song is taken from the "Amphion Anglicus," published in 1700.

I pass all my hours.

ANOTHER of the first set of Children of the Chapel Royal on its reëstablishment was Pelham Humfrey, as he spelled it himself, though it is more often spelled Humphrey. In 1664, when seventeen years of age, he was sent abroad by Charles II to study, which he did chiefly in Paris, under Lully. He returned to England in 1667, and in Pepys' Diary there is an amusing glimpse of him.

"November 15. Home, and there find, as I expected, Mr. Cæsar and little Pelham Humfreys, lately returned from France, and is an absolute Monsieur, as full of form and confidence and vanity, and disparages everything and everybody's skill but his own." According to Hawkins, on Humfrey's arrival Captain Cooke at once took to his bed and died of envy. However that may be, Humfrey became the Master of the Children in 1672, and died in 1674. He showed great promise rather than performance, but nevertheless left several fine anthems, some odes and many songs. He was also one of the first lute-players of his day.

"I pass all my hours" has an added interest from the fact that the words are by Pelham's royal patron and master, Charles II.

Henry Purcell.

HENRY PURCELL, like Henry Lawes, came of a thoroughly musical family, his father and uncle being gentlemen of the Chapel Royal, while his brother, son and grandson were all musicians. He was born in 1658 or 1659, there being no exact record of the date, and on his father's death in 1664 he was adopted by his uncle, and appointed a chorister of the Chapel Royal.

He succeeded Blow as organist of Westminster in 1680, and in this year were performed "Theodosius" and "The Virtuous Wife," the first of the many dramatic works for which he wrote music. Sometimes the music in these consisted of only a song or two, sometimes it was a complete opera; but all the works were formerly classed as "operas," and so gave an exaggerated idea of Purcell's fertility, which was great enough to need no exaggeration. These "operas" alone number over fifty, the most important of them being "King Arthur," "Dido and Æneas," "The Fairy Queen," "The Indian Queen," etc.

Besides this, Purcell composed over seventy anthems, half a dozen services, many hymns, odes and "Welcome Songs," which were occasional works written to welcome his royal master or mistress on their return from visits to the continent. Moreover, he wrote many separate songs, scattered through various collections, and a quantity of instrumental music. As he died in his thirty-seventh year, this enormous output testifies sufficiently to his industry and fertility.

By the time he was twenty Purcell was recognized by his contemporaries as the first English musician of his time, and looking back from this distance we see clearly that he was the greatest and most original genius that England has ever produced in music. It has been claimed for him that he invented the English song, but from what we have seen in this volume that claim can hardly be sustained. But, as Mr. Duncan truly says, he had a "fine dramatic instinct when musicians the world over were obsessed by the splendid stupidity of scholastic counterpoint."

His influence has been great and lasting. Händel in particular must have been a diligent student of Purcell's works, and it is not too much to say that if there had never been a Purcell, there would never have been the Händel whom we know. The difference between the Händel of Italian opera and the Händel of oratorio, and the resemblance between Händel's later music and Purcell's, are too great to have been fortuitous.

Purcell's early death in 1695 was the greatest loss which English music ever suffered, and his epitaph in Westminster Abbey is no hollow compliment.

"Here lyes HENRY PURCELL, Esqr., who left this Life and is gone to that Blessed Place where only his Harmony can be exceeded."

Of the songs in this collection, the Knotting Song was found by Mr. William H. Cummings, the distinguished authority on English music, pasted in the lid of an old workbox. "Lilliburlero," as has already been said, is a song satirizing the Catholics, composed at the end of the reign of James II, and it instantly gained a popularity which ran from one end of the country to the other. It was one of the potent influences in losing the crown for the last of the Stuart kings.

Daniel Purcell. DANIEL PURCELL, younger brother of the great Henry, seems to have been born about 1660, for the record of his birth is as imperfect as his brother's. Little is known of his early life, but in 1688 he was appointed organist of Magdalen College, Oxford, where he remained till 1695, when he came to London, perhaps on account of his brother's illness and death.

From this time Daniel Purcell seems to have been much in demand as a writer of dramatic music, for he composed the music for a number of plays and masques. He also wrote many songs, glees, etc. He died in 1717.

Henricus Purcell.
Ætat Suæ 37.

Contents

Index of First Lines

RELIQUARY OF ENGLISH SONGS

Summer is a-coming in
(Sumer is icumen in)

About A.D. 1250

Copyright, 1915, by G. Schirmer

Ah! the syghes that come fro' my heart

Time of Henry VII

Tenderly

1. Ah! the syghes that come fro' my heart, They
2. I was wont her to___ be-hold, And

grieve   me pass - ing   sore,_____   Syth   I   must fro' my
take   in arm - es   twain,_____   And   now,   with sygh - es

love   de - part,   Fare - well,   my joye, for ev - er - more._____
man - i - fold,   Fare - well,   my joye! and welcome   pain!_____

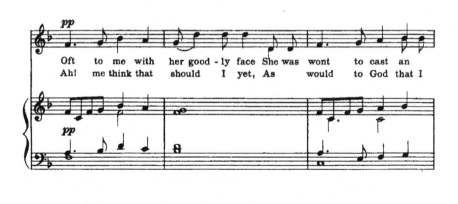

Oft to me with her good-ly face She was wont to cast an
Ah! me think that should I yet, As would to God that I

eye,_____ But now ab-sence to me_ in_ place; A-
might!_____ There would no joys com - pare with it Un -

las! for woe I die, I die._____
to my heart, to make it light._____

24814

Pastime with good company

Henry VIII
(1491-1547)

Sturdy and bright

1. Pas - time with good
2. Youth will needs have
3. Com - pan - y with

com - pan - y I love, and shall un - til__ I die;
dal - li - ance, Of good or ill, some pas - tance;
hon - est - y Is vir - tue sure; and vice to flee,

Grudge who will, but none__ de - ny So
Com - pan - y me think - eth the best All
Com - pan - y, is good__ or ill, But

God be pleas'd, this life—will I For my pas-tance, Hunt,
thoughts and fan - ta - sies to di - gest; For i - dle - ness Is
ev - 'ry man has his—free will. The best I sue, The

sing, and dance; My heart is— set, All good -ly sport, To
chief mis -tress Of vic - es— all: Then who can say But
worst es - chew; My mind shall be Vir - tue to use, Vice

my com - fort, Who shall— me————— let?
pass the day Is best— of————— all?
to re - fuse, I shall— use————— me.

The Hunt is up

Time of Henry VIII

1. The Hunt is up,— the Hunt is up,— And
it— is well— nigh day,— And Har-ry our king is
gone— hunt-ing To bring— his deer— to bay.—

The Hunt is up

I

The Hunt is up, the Hunt is up,
  And it is well nigh day,
And Harry our king is gone hunting
  To bring his deer to bay.

II

The East is bright with morning light,
  And darkness it is fled;
The merry horn wakes up the morn
  To leave his idle bed.

III

Behold, the skies with golden dyes
  Are glowing all around;
The grass is green, so are the treen
  All laughing at the sound.

IV

The horses snort to see the sport,
  The dogs are running free,
The woods rejoice at the merry noise
  Of hey tantara, tee ree!

V

The sun is glad to see us clad
  All in our lusty green,
And smiles in sky as he riseth high
  To see and to be seen.

VI

Awake, all men, I say again,
  Be merry as you may
For Harry our king is gone hunting
  To bring his deer to bay.

14814

You Gentlemen of England

Words by Martin Packer

Tune, time of Elizabeth

1. You gen-tle-men of Eng - land, Who live at home at ease, How lit -tle do you think up-on The dan-gers of the seas: Give ear un-to the mar - i -ners, And they will plain - ly show_ All_ the

Chorus

cares and the fears, When the storm-y winds do blow; All the

cares and the fears, When the storm-y winds do blow.

You Gentlemen of England

I

You gentlemen of England,
 Who live at home at ease,
How little do you think upon
 The dangers of the seas:
Give ear unto the mariners,
 And they will plainly show
||:All the cares and the fears
 When the stormy winds do blow.:||

II

All you that will be seamen,
 Must bear a valiant heart,
For when you come upon the seas,
 You must not think to start,
Nor once to be faint-hearted
 In hail, rain, blow or snow,
||:Nor to think for to shrink
 When the stormy winds do blow.:||

III

Sometimes in Neptune's bosom
 Our ship is toss'd by waves,
And every man expecting
 The sea to be our graves;
Then up again she's mounted
 And down again so low,
||:In the waves, on the seas,
 When the stormy winds do blow.:||

IV

But when the danger's over,
 And safe we come on shore,
The horrors of the tempest,
 We think of them no more;
The flowing bowl invites us,
 And joyfully we go,
||:All the day drink away,
 Tho' the stormy winds do blow.:||

The Three Ravens

Time of Elizabeth

1. There were three ra'ens sat on a tree,

Down a down hey, down a down, There were three ra'ens sat on a tree, With a

down; There were three ra'ens sat on a tree, They were as black as

they might be, With a down derry, der-ry, der-ry down down. *After last verse*

24814

The Three Ravens

I

There were three ra'ens sat on a tree,
Down a down, hey, down a down,
There were three ra'ens sat on a tree,
With a down;
There were three ra'ens sat on a tree,
They were as black as they might be,
With a down, derry, derry, derry down down.

II

Then one of them said to his mate,
O where shall we our breakfast take?

III

Down in yonder green field
There lies a knight slain 'neath his shield.

IV

His hounds they lie down at his feet,
So well do they their master keep.

V

His hawks they fly so eagerly,
There's no fowl that dare come him nigh.

VI

Down there comes a fallow doe,
As great with young as she might go.

VII

She lifted up his bloody head,
And kiss'd his wounds that were so red.

VIII

She got him upon her back,
And carried him to earthern lake.

IX

She buried him before the prime;
She was dead herself ere eventime.

X

God send to every gentleman
Such hawks, and hounds, and such a leman.

I Live Not Where I Love

Time of Elizabeth

com-men-da-tion of my love, Re - solv - ing ev - er to part nev-er,

Though I live not where I love.

I Live Not Where I Love

I

Loyal lovers, that are distant
  From your sweethearts many a mile,
Pray come and help me at this instant
  In mirth to spend away the while;
Singing sweetly and completely
  In commendation of my love,
Resolving ever to part never,
  Though I live not where I love.

II

My constancy shall ne'er be failing
  Whatsoe'er betide me here,
Of her virtue I'll be telling
  Be my biding far or near.
And though blind fortune prove uncertain
  From her presence me to remove,
Yet I'll be constant every instant,
  Though I live not where I love.

III

Though our bodies thus are parted,
  And asunder many a mile,
Yet I vow to be true-hearted
  And be faithful all the while.
Though with mine eye I cannot spy
  For distance great my dearest love,
My heart is with her altogether,
  Though I live not where I love.

IV

The birds shall leave their airy region,
  The fishes in the air shall fly,
All the world shall be at one religion,
  All living things shall cease to die.
All things shall change to shapes most strange,
  Above that I disloyal prove,
Or any way my love decay,
  Though I live not where I love.

It was a lover and his lass

Words by Shakespeare

Thomas Morley
(1557-1604)

Now is the month of maying

Thomas Morley

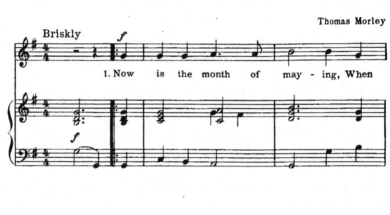

1. Now   is   the   month   of   may - ing, When

mer - ry   lads   are   play - ing;   Fa   la   la   la   la   la

la   la   la!   Fa   la   la   la   la   la   la!   Each   with   his   bon - ny

lass, A - danc-ing on the grass, Fa la

la la la! Fa la la la la la la la la la la la!

Each verse may be repeated **pp**

Now is the month of maying

I

Now is the month of maying,
When merry lads are playing;
Fa la la la la la la la!
Fa la la la la la la!
Each with his bonny lass
A-dancing on the grass.
Fa la la la la!
Fa la la la la la la, la la la la la!

II

The Spring, clad all in gladness,
Doth laugh at Winter's sadness;
And to the bagpipes' sound
The Nymphs tread out their round.

III

Fie, then, why sit we musing,
Youth's sweet delight refusing?
Say, dainty nymphs, and speak,
Shall we play barley-break?

The Willow Song

Time of Elizabeth

Slowly and sadly

The poor soul sat sigh-ing by a syc-a-more tree, Sing all a green wil-low; Her hand on her bo-som, her head on her knee; Sing

The British Grenadiers

Time of Elizabeth

1. Some talk of Al - ex - an - der, And some of Her - cu - les, Of Hec-tor and Ly - sa - der, And such great names as these; But of all the world's brave he - roes, There's

none that can com - pare,_____ With a tow row row row

row row, To the Brit-ish Gren-a - dier.

The British Grenadiers

I

Some talk of Alexander, and some of Hercules,
Of Hector and Lysander, and such great names
as these;
But of all the world's brave heroes there's none
that can compare
With a tow, row, row, row, row, row to the
British Grenadier.

II

Those heroes of antiquity ne'er faced a cannonball,
Or knew the force of powder to stay their foes
withal;
But our brave boys do know it, and banish all
their fears
With a tow, row, row, row, row, row for the
British Grenadiers.

III

Whene'er we are commanded to storm the
palisades,
Our leaders march with fuses, and we with
hand-grenades,
We throw them from the glacis about the
enemy's ears:
Sing tow, row, row, row, row, row for the
British Grenadiers.

IV

And when the siege is over, we to the town repair,
The townsmen cry, Hurra, boys, here comes a
Grenadier!
Here come the Grenadiers, my boys, who know
no doubts nor fears.
Then sing tow, row, row, row, row, row for the
British Grenadiers.

V

Then let us fill a bumper, and drink a health to
those
Who carry caps and pouches, and wear the
loupèd clothes.
May they and their commanders live happy all
their years,
With a tow, row, row, row, row, row for the
British Grenadiers.

Love will find out the way

Time of Elizabeth

1. O - ver the mountains And o - ver the waves; Un - der the foun - tains And un - der the graves; Un - der floods that are deep-est, Which Nep-tune o - bey; O-ver rocks that are steep-est, Love will find out the way.

Love will find out the way

I

Over the mountains
  And over the waves;
Under the fountains
  And under the graves;
Under floods that are deepest,
  Which Neptune obey,
Over rocks that are steepest,
  Love will find out the way.

II

Where there is no place
  For the glow-worm to lie;
Where there is no place
  For receipt of a fly;
Where the midge dares not venture,
  Lest herself fast she lay,
If Love come, he will enter,
  And soon find out his way.

III

You may esteem him
  A child for his might;
Or you may deem him
  A coward from his flight;
But if she whom Love doth honour
  Be conceal'd from the day,
Set a thousand guards upon her,
  Love will find out the way.

IV

Some think to lose him
  By having him confin'd;
Some do suppose him,
  Poor thing, to be blind;
But if ne'er so close you wall him,
  Do the best that you may,
Blind Love, if so ye call him,
  Soon will find out his way.

V

You may train the eagle
  To stoop to your fist;
You may inveigle
  The Phœnix of the East;
The lioness, you may move her
  To give o'er her prey;
But you'll ne'er stop a lover:
  He will find out the way.

What if a day

Time of Elizabeth

1. What if a day, or a month, or a year, Crown thy de-lights with a
2. Earth's but a point of the world, and a man Is but a point of the

thousand sweet con-tent -ings, a thousand sweet con - tent - ings?
Earth's compar - ed cen -tre, the Earth's compar - ed cen - tre;

May not the change of a night or an hour Cross thy delights with as
Shall then the point of a point be so vain, As to triumph in a

many sad tormentings, as man-y sad tor - ment - ings? For - tune, hon-our,
sil-ly point's ad-venture, a sil - ly point's ad - ven - ture? All in haz-ard

beau - ty, youth, Are but blossoms dy - ing; Wan - ton pleasure,
that we have, Here is nothing bid - ing; Days of pleasure

dot - ing love, Are but shad-ows fly - ing. All our joys
are as streams Thro' fair meadows glid - ing. Weal or woe,

are but toys, I - dle thoughts de - ceiv - ing, None hath pow'r
time doth go, Time hath no re - turn - ing; Se - cret fates

of an hour Of the life's be - reav - ing.
guide our states Both in mirth and mourn-ing.

24814

Have you seen but a white lily grow

Words by Ben Jonson

Time of James 1

swan's down ev-er? Or have smelt of the bud of the bri-ar? Or the

nard of the fire? Or have tast-ed the bag of the bee? O so white, O so

soft, O so sweet is she, so sweet is she; O so

white, O so soft, O so sweet, so sweet,— so sweet is she.

Awake, sweet love

John Dowland
(1562-1626)

Smoothly and cheerfully

1. Awake, sweet love, thou art re - turn'd! My heart, which long in
2. If she es - teem thee, now, aught worth, She will not grieve thy

ab - sence mourn'd, Lives now in per - fect day.
love hence-forth, Which so despair hath prov'd.

Let love, which nev - er ab - sent dies, Now live for ev - er
Despair hath prov - ed now in me That love will not in -

in her eyes, Whence came my first an - noy.
con - stant be, Tho' long in vain I lov'd.

On-ly her-self   hath seem - ed fair, She on-ly   I   could love,
If she at last   re - ward   thy love, And all thy harms   re - pair,

She on-ly drove me to de - spair, When she un - kind did prove.
Thy happi-ness will sweeter   prove, Rais'd up from deep de - spair.

Despair did make me wish me die, That I my griefs might end;
And if that now   thou wel - come be When thou with her   dost meet,

She on-ly which did make me   fly, My state may now a - mend.
She, all this while, but play'd with   thee, To make thy joys more   sweet.

Come again, sweet love

John Dowland

gain,   Sweet love doth now in - vite   Thy
gain,   That I may cease to mourn   Thro'

grac-es that re - frain   To   do me due de - light,   To see,__
thy un - kind dis - dain;   For now, left and for - lorn,   I sit,__

24814

Now, O now I needs must part

John Dowland

Once I loved a maiden fair

Time of James I

In moderate time

1. Once I lov'd a maiden fair, But she did de-ceive me; She with Ve-nus might compare

In my mind, be-lieve me. She was young and among Creatures of temp-

ta - tion; Who will say but maidens may   Kiss for rec-re - a - tion?

Once I loved a maiden fair

I

Once I loved a maiden fair,
  But she did deceive me;
She with Venus might compare,
  In my mind, believe me.
She was young, and among
  Creatures of temptation;
Who will say but maidens may
  Kiss for recreation!

II

Three times I did make it known
  To the congregation
That the Church should make us one,
  As priest had made relation.
Married we straight must be,
  Although we go a-begging;
Now, alas! 'tis like to prove
  A very hopeless wedding.

III

Happy he who never knew
  What to love belongèd;
Maidens wav'ring and untrue
  Many a man have wrongèd.
Fare thee well, faithless girl,
  I'll not sorrow for thee;
Once I held thee dear as pearl,
  Now I do abhor thee.

Tobacco's but an Indian weed

Words by George Wither

Time of James I

1. To - bac - co's but an In - dian weed, Grows green at morn, cut down at_ eve, It shews our de - cay, We_ are_ but_ clay: Think of this when you smoke to - bac - co.

Tobacco's but an Indian weed

I

Tobacco's but an Indian weed,
Grows green at morn, cut down at eve;
    It shews our decay,
    We are but clay:
Think of this, when you smoke tobacco.

II

The pipe that is so lily-white,
Wherein so many take delight,
    Is broke with a touch,
    Man's life is such:
Think of this, when you smoke tobacco.

III

The pipe that is so foul within
Shews how man's soul is stained with sin;
    It doth require
    To be purged with fire:
Think of this, when you smoke tobacco.

IV

The ashes that are left behind
Do serve to put us all in mind
    That unto dust
    Return we must:
Think of this, when you smoke tobacco.

V

The smoke, that does so high ascend,
Doth shew man's life must have an end;
    The vapour's gone,
    Man's life is done:
Think of this, when you smoke tobacco.

Phillida and Coridon

Time of James I

would have kiss'd her then, She said maids must kiss no men, Till they
man - y a pret - ty oath, As yea and nay, and faith and troth, Such as

kiss for good and all; Then she bade the shep - herd call All the
sil - ly shepherds use, When they would not love a - buse; Love which

p

cresc. *rit.* 3. Close, 4th verse

gods to wit-ness truth Ne'er was lov'd so fair a youth.
had been long de - lud-ed, Was with kiss-es sweet con - cluded: And Philli-

cresc. *rit.* *f*

rit.

da with garlands gay Was crown - ed the La - dy May.

rit.

24814

Wronge not, deare Empress of my hearte

Time of Charles I
Harmonized by T. Tertius Noble

1. Wronge not, deare Empress of my hearte, The mer-rits of true pas-sion, By thinkinge that hee feels noe smarte Who su-eth for noe com-pas-sion; Since that my playnts doe not ap-prove

The con - quest of your bew-tie, It comes not from the ef-

fect of __ love, But __ from ex - ces - sive du - ty.

Wronge not, deare Empress of my hearte

I

Wronge not, deare Empress of my hearte,
  The merrits of true passion,
By thinkinge that hee feels noe smarte
  Who sueth for noe compassion.
Since that my playnts doe not approve
  The conquest of your bewtie,
It comes not from the effect of love,
  But from excessive duty.

II

That knowinge that I sue to serve
  A sainte of such perfection,
Whom all desires, but none deserves
  A place in her affection:
I rather chuse to want relief
  Than utter the revealinge;
When glory recommendes the griefe,
  Despaire dissuades the healinge.

III

Thus those desires that ayme to high,
  Of any mortall lover,
When reason cannot make them dye,
  Discretion must them cover:
But when discretion doth bereave
  The playnte which they should utter,
Then theyre discretion might perceave
  That silence is a suter.

IV

Silence in love doth shew more love
  Than words, though nere so witty,
The beggar that is dumbe, you knowe,
  Deservès double pitty.
Then wronge not, deare hearte of my hearte,
  My true harts secret passion;
He smarteth most, that hides his smarte
  And sueth for noe compassion.

Why should'st thou swear I am forsworn

Charles I

Smoothly and with expression

mf

1. Why should'st thou

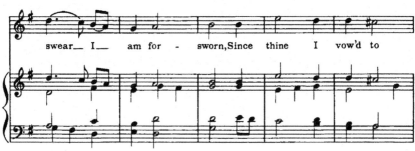

swear␣ I␣ am for - sworn, Since thine I vow'd to

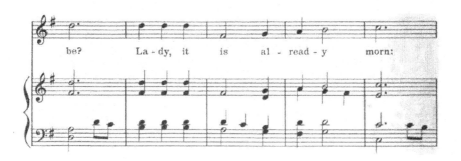

be? La - dy, it is al - read - y morn:

24814

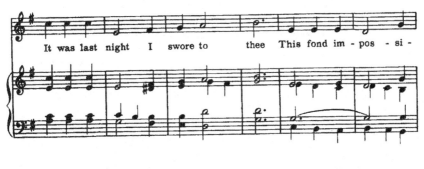

It was last night I swore to thee This fond im - pos - si -

bil - i - ty.

Why should'st thou swear
I am forsworn

I

Why should'st thou swear I am forsworn,
   Since thine I vow'd to be?
Lady, it is already morn:
    It was last night I swore to thee
    This fond impossibility.

II

Have I not lov'd thee much and long,
   A tedious twelve hours' space!
I should all other beauties wrong
   And rob thee of a new embrace,
   Should I still dote upon thy face.

III

Not that all joys in thy brown hair
   By others may be found;
But I will search the dark, the fair,
   Like skilful min'ralists that found
   Their treasures in unploughèd ground.

Phillis, on the new-made hay

Time of Charles I

Cheerfully

mf

cresc.

mp

mp

1. Phil - lis, on the new-made hay, In re - clin - ing

pos - ture lay, Wast - ing all the sum - mer day In

mel - an - chol - y dream - ing. Phil - lis, drive your

After last verse

Phillis, on the new-made hay

I

Phillis, on the new-made hay,
In reclining posture lay,
Wasting all the summer day
    In melancholy dreaming.
Phillis, drive your cares away
    While June's bright sun is beaming.

II

False Amintas, so she thought,
Fair-haired Chloë's cottage sought,
And a store of roses brought,
    The maiden's birthday greeting.
"Shepherd, is thy promise nought?"
    Are lover's vows so fleeting?

III

"Can you thus scorn Cupid's yoke?
Can your face such falsehood cloke?"
Thus in dreaming Phillis spoke,
    Her idle fears revealing;
Fond Amintas, when she woke,
    She found beside her kneeling.

Sally in Our Alley

Words by Henry Carey

Tune, time of Charles I

al-ley.

Sally in Our Alley

I

Of all the girls that are so smart,
  There's none like pretty Sally,
She is the darling of my heart
  And lives in our alley.
There's ne'er a lady in the land
  That's half so sweet as Sally,
She is the darling of my heart,
  And lives in our alley.

II

Her father he makes cabbage nets
  And through the streets does cry them;
Her mother she sells laces long
  To such as please to buy them;
But sure such folks could ne'er beget
  So sweet a girl as Sally;
She is the darling of my heart,
  And lives in our alley.

III

When she is by, I leave my work,
  I love her so sincerely;
My master comes, like any Turk,
  And bangs me most severely:
But let him bang, long as he will,
  I'll bear it all for Sally;
She is the darling of my heart,
  And lives in our alley.

IV

Of all the days are in the week
  I dearly love but one day,
And that's the day that comes betwixt
  A Saturday and Monday:
For then I'm drest in all my best
  To walk abroad with Sally;
She is the darling of my heart,
  And lives in our alley.

V

My master carries me to church,
  And often I am blamèd,
Because I leave him in the lurch,
  Soon as the text is namèd.
I leave the church in sermon-time,
  And slink away to Sally;
She is the darling of my heart,
  And lives in our alley.

VI

When Christmas comes about again,
  O then I shall have money,
I'll hoard it up, and box and all
  I'll give unto my honey:
I would it were ten thousand pounds;
  I'd give it all to Sally,
She is the darling of my heart,
  And lives in our alley.

VII

My master and the neighbors all
  Make game of me and Sally,
And but for her I'd better be
  A slave and row a galley.
But when my sev'n long years are out,
  Oh! then I'll marry Sally:
She is the darling of my heart,
  And lives in our alley.

Come, lovely Phillis

Henry Lawes
(1595-1640)

In moderate time

1. Come, love-ly Phil - lis, Since it thy will is, To crown thy Cor - ri-don with daf - fo - dil-lies; With man-y kiss - es, As sweet as this is, I will re - pay to mul - ti-ply thy bliss-es.

Here I will hold thee, And thus en - fold thee, Free from

harms with - in these___ arms.

Come, lovely Phillis

I

Come, lovely Phillis,
Since it thy will is
To crown thy Coridon with daffodillies;
With many kisses
As sweet as this is
I will repay to multiply thy blisses.
Here I will hold thee,
And thus enfold thee,
Free from harms within these arms.

II

Sweet, still be smiling,
'Tis sweet beguiling
Of tedious hours and sorrow's best exiling;
For if you lower
The banks no power
Will have to bring forth any pleasant flower.
Your eyes not granting
Their rays enchanting,
Mine may reign, but 'twere in vain.

About the sweet bag of a bee

Henry Lawes

Which Ve-nus hear-ing, thith-er came And for their bold-ness stript them,

And taking thence from each his flame, With rods of myr-tle whipt them.

Slower

Which done, to still their wan-ton crys, And qui-et grown she'd seen them,

Tenderly

She kiss'd and dried their dove-like eyes And gave the bag between them.

How happy art thou

Henry Lawes

Briskly *mf*

1. How hap - py art thou and I, That nev - er knew how to love! There's no such bless - ing here be - neath, What - e'er there is a - bove. 'Tis

lib - er - ty, 'tis   lib - er - ty, That   ev - 'ry wise   man   knows.

How happy art thou

I

How happy art thou and I,
  That never knew how to love!
There's no such blessing here beneath,
  Whate'er there is above.
'Tis liberty, 'tis liberty,
  That every wise man knows.

II

Out, out upon those eyes
  That think to murder me,
And he's an ass believes her fair
  That is not kind and free.
There's nothing sweet, there's nothing sweet
  To man but liberty.

III

I'll tie my heart to none,
  Nor yet confine mine eyes,
But I will play my game so well
  I'll never want a prize.
'Tis liberty, 'tis liberty
  Has made me now thus wise.

If the quick spirit of your eye

Henry Lawes

fly from that for - sak - en face,
your fresh beau - ty ev - er fade;

Quicker

Then, Ce - lia, let___ us___ reap___ our joys, Ere time such
Then, Ce - lia, fear___ not to___ be - stow What still, being

After second Verse

good - ly fruit____ de - stroys. Thus ei - ther Time his
ga - ther'd, still____ must grow.

sick - le brings In vain___ or___ else in vain his wings.

Phillis, why should we delay

Henry Lawes

Moderate time

1. Phil - lis, why should we_ de - lay Plea - sures shorter than the day? Could we, which we nev - er can, Stretch our lives be - yond their span, Beau - ty like a shad - ow flies, And our youth be - fore us dies.

24814

Phillis, why should we delay

I

Phillis, why should we delay
Pleasures shorter than the day?
Could we, which we never can,
Stretch our lives beyond their span,
Beauty like a shadow flies
And our youth before us dies.

II

Or would youth and beauty stay, ˙
Love has wings and will away;
Love has swifter wings than time,
Change in love too oft do's chime;
Gods, that never change their state,
Vary of their love and hate.

III

Phillis, to this truth we owe
All the love betwixt us now;
Let not you and I inquire
What has been our past desire;
On what shepherds you have smil'd,
Or what nymphs I have beguil'd.

Beauty and Love

Henry Lawes

Thou hast no pow'r o'er men at all, But what I gave to thee,

rit.

Nor art thou long - er fair or sweet, Than men acknow-ledge me.

Beauty and Love

I

Beauty and Love once fell at odds,
  And thus revil'd each other,
Quoth Love, I am one of the gods,
  And you wait on my mother.
Thou hast no pow'r o'er men at all,
  But what I gave to thee,
Nor art thou longer fair and sweet
  Than men acknowledge me.

II

Away, fond boy! then Beauty said,
  We see that thou art blind,
But men have knowing eyes and can
  My graces better find.
'Twas I begot thee, mortals know,
  And call'd thee blind desire;
I made thy arrows and thy bow
  And wings to kindle fire.

III

Love here in rage flew away,
  And straight to Vulcan pray'd
That he would tip his shafts with scorn,
  To punish this proud maid:
So Beauty ever since hath been
  But courted for an hour,
To love a day is now a sin
  'Gainst Cupid and his pow'r.

I do confess

Henry Lawes

1. I do con - fess th'art smooth and fair And I might ha' gone near to love thee, Had I not found the slight - est pray'r That lips could say_ had pow'r to move thee: But I can let thee

now a - lone, As wor - thy to___ be lov'd by none.

I do confess

I

I do confess th'art smooth and fair
  And I might ha' gone near to love thee,
Had I not found the slightest pray'r
  That lips could say had pow'r to move thee:
    But I can let thee now alone,
    As worthy to be lov'd by none.

II

I do confess th'art sweet, yet find
  Thee such an unthrift of thy sweets,
Thy favours are but like the wind,
  Which kisseth ev'rything it meets;
    And since thou canst with more than one,
    Th'art worthy to be kiss'd by none.

III

The morning rose, that untouch'd stands
  With briars arm'd, how sweet she smells!
But pluck'd, and strain'd through ruder hands,
  Her sweets no longer with her dwells:
    But scent and beauty both are gone,
    And leaves fall from her one by one.

IV

Such fate ere long will thee betide,
  When thou hast handled been a while,
With sere flow'rs to be thrown aside;
  And I shall sigh when some will smile
    To see thy love to ev'ry one
    Hath brought thee to be lov'd by none.

Little love serves my turn

Henry Lawes

1. Lit - tle love serves my turn,
2. Beau - ty shall court it - self,

'Tis   so   en - flam - - ing,   Ra - ther than   I   will burn,
'Tis   not worth speak - ing,   I'll   no   more   a - mor - ous

I   will_ leave gam - - ing: For when   I   think up - on't,
pangs, No more heart - break - - ing: Those that ne'er felt   the smart,

O, 'tis so pain - ful, 'Cause la - dies have a trick To be dis-dain-ful.
Let them go try   it,   I   have re-deem'd my heart, Now I de - fy it.

No more, no more!   I must give o'er, For beau - ty is so____ sweet,
For - give me, love,   if I re-move In - to some oth - er____ sphere

It makes me pine, dis - tracts the mind, And sur - feits when I____ see't.
Where I may keep a   flock of sheep, And know no oth - er____ care.

24814

I prethee, send me back my heart

Henry Lawes

Tenderly

1. I pre-thee, send me back my heart, Since I can-not have thine; For if from yours you will not part, Why then should you keep mine?

I prethee, send me back my heart

I

I prethee, send me back my heart,
    Since I cannot have thine;
For if from yours you will not part,
    Why then should you keep mine!

II

Yet now I think on't, let it lie,
    To send it me were vain,
For th'hast a thief in either eye,
    Will steal it back again!

III

Why should two hearts in one breast lie,
    And yet not lodge together?
O love! where is thy sympathy,
    If thus our hearts thou sever?

IV

But love is such a mystery,
    I cannot find it out;
For when I think I'm best resolv'd,
    I then am most in doubt.

V

Then farewell care and farewell woe,
    I will no longer pine,
But I'll believe I have her heart
    As much as she has mine.

Gather ye rosebuds

Herrick

William Lawes

1. Ga-ther ye rose-buds while you may, Old

Time is still a__ fly-ing, And that same flow'r that smiles to - day To-mor-row

will be dy-ing.

Gather ye rosebuds
while you may

I

Gather ye rosebuds while you may,
  Old Time is still a-flying,
And that same flow'r that smiles to-day
  To-morrow will be dying.

II

The glorious lamp of heav'n, the Sun,
  The higher he is getting,
The sooner will his race be run,
  And nearer he's to setting.

III

That age is best that is the first,
  While youth and blood are warmer;
But being spent the worse and worst,
  Times still succeeds the former.

IV

Then be not coy, but use your time,
  And while you may, go marry,
For having once but lost your prime,
  You may for ever tarry.

Wert thou more fairer than thou art

J. Wilson

1. Wert thou more

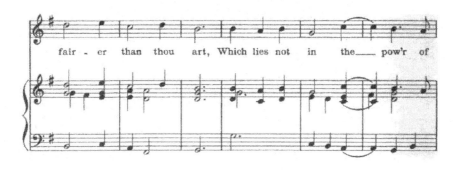

fair - er than thou art, Which lies not in the____ pow'r of

Art, Or had'st thou in thine____ eyes more darts, Than ev - er

24814

Cu - pid____ shot at hearts: Yet, if they were____ not

shot____ at me, I should not cast____ a____ thought on thee.

Wert thou more fairer
than thou art

I

Wert thou more fairer than thou art,
Which lies not in the pow'r of art,
Or had'st thou in thine eyes more darts
Than Cupid ever shot at hearts:
Yet, if they were not shot at me,
I should not cast a thought on thee.

II

I'd rather marry a disease
Than court the thing I cannot please;
She that would cherish my desires,
Must court my flame with equal fires:
What pleasure is there in a kiss
To him that doubt's the heart's not his?

III

I love thee not because thou'rt fair,
Softer than down, smoother than air,
Not for the cupids that doth lie
In either corner of thine eye:
Would you then know what it might be?
'Tis I love you, 'cause you love me.

When the King enjoys his own again

Words by
Martin Parker

Tune, time of Charles I

Briskly and boldly

What *Book - er* can prog - nos - ti - cate Con -

cern - ing kings' or king - doms' fate? I think my - self to

Barbara Allen

1. In Scar-let Town, where I was born; There was a fair maid dwell-in', Made

ev-'ry youth cry Well-a-day? Her name was Bar-b'ra Al-len.

Barbara Allen

I

In Scarlet Town, where I was born,
  There was a fair maid dwellin',
Made ev'ry youth cry, Well-a-day?
  Her name was Barbara Allen.

II

All in the merry month of May,
  When green buds they were swellin',
Young Jemmy Grove on his death-bed lay,
  For love of Barbara Allen.

III

He sent his man unto her then,
  To the town where she was dwellin';
You must come to my master dear,
  Giff your name be Barbara Allen.

IV

For death is printed on his face,
  And o'er his heart is stealin';
Then haste away to comfort him,
  O lovely Barbara Allen.

V

Though death be printed on his face
  And o'er his heart is stealin',
Yet little better shall he be
  For bonny Barbara Allen.

VI

So slowly, slowly, she came up,
  And slowly she came nigh him,
And all she said, when there she came,
  Young man, I think you're dying.

VII

He turned his face unto her straight,
  With deadly sorrow sighing;
O lovely maid, come pity me,
  I'm on my death-bed lying.

VIII

If on your death-bed you do lie,
  What needs the tale you're tellin';
I cannot keep you from your death;
  Farewell, said Barbara Allen.

*   *   *   *   *   *   *

XIII

When he was dead and laid in grave,
  Her heart was struck with sorrow,
O mother, mother, make my bed,
  For I shall die to-morrow.

XIV

Hard-hearted creature him to slight,
  Who lovèd me so dearly;
O that I had been more kind to him
  When he was alive and near me!

XV

She, on her death-bed as she lay,
  Begg'd to be buried by him;
And sore repented of the day,
  That she did e'er deny him.

XVI

Farewell, she said, ye virgins all,
  And shun the fault I fell in:
Henceforth take warning by the fall
  Of cruel Barbara Allen.

The Self-banished

Words by
Edmund Waller

Dr. Blow
(1648-1708)

In moderate time

It is not that I love you less Than when be-

fore___ your feet I lay; But to pre - vent___ the

sad in - crease Of hope - less love I keep a - way.

24814

I pass all my hours

Words by Charles II

Pelham Humphrey

- ing   too   well.

l.h.

I pass all my hours

I

I pass all my hours in a shady old grove,
But I live not the day when I see not my love;
I survey ev'ry walk, now my Phillis is gone,
And sigh when I think we were there all alone.
O then 'tis, O then, that I think there's no hell
    Like loving too well.

II

But each shade and each conscious bow'r when
    I find
Where I once have been happy, and she has been
    kind;
When I see the print of her shape in the green
And imagine the pleasure may yet come again:
O then 'tis I think that no joys are above
    The pleasures of love.

III

While alone to myself I repeat all her charms,
She I love may be lock'd in another man's arms,
She may laugh at my cares, and so false she may
    be,
To say the kind things she before said to me.
O then 'tis, O then, that I think there's no hell
    Like loving too well.

IV

But when I consider the truth of her heart,
Such an innocent passion, so kind without art,
I much fear I have wronged her, and hope she
    may be
So full of true love to be jealous of me:
And then 'tis I think that no joys are above
    The pleasures of love.

The Knotting Song

Henry Purcell
(1658 - 1695)

24814

Sat___ and knot-ted, and knot-ted, and knot-ted, and knot-ted

all the while.

The Knotting Song

I

Hears not my Phillis how the birds
   Their feather'd mates salute?
They tell their passion in their words:
   Must I alone be mute?
     Phillis, without a frown or smile,
     Sat and knotted all the while.

II

So many months in silence past,
   And yet in raging love,
Might well deserve one word at last,
   My passion should approve?
     Phillis, without a frown or smile,
     Sat and knotted all the while.

III

Must then your faithful swain expire,
   And not one look obtain,
Which he in sooth his fond desire
   Might pleasingly explain?
     Phillis, without a frown or smile,
     Sat and knotted all the while.

Lilliburlero

Words by Lord Wharton

Henry Purcell

le ~ ro, lil-li-bur ~ le ~ ro, le ~ ro, le ~ ro bul-len a ~ la!

Lilliburlero

I

Ho! broder Teague, dost hear de decree,
Lilliburlero bullen a la!
Dat we shall have a new deputie?
Lilliburlero bullen a la!
Lero lero, lilliburlero, lero lero, bullen a la!
Lero lero, lilliburlero, lero lero, bullen a la!

II

Ho! by shaint Tyburn, it is de Talbote,
And he will cut all de English troate.

III

Dough by my shoul de English do praat,
De law's on dare side, and Creish knows what.

IV

But if dispence do come from de pope,
We'll hang Magna Charta, and dem in a rope.

V

For de good Talbot is made a lord,
And with brave lads is coming aboard:

VI

Who in all France have taken a sware,
Dat dey will have no Protestant heir.

VII

Ara! but why does he stay behind?
Ho! by my shoul 'tis a Protestant wind.

VIII

But see, de Tyrconnel is now come ashore,
And we shall have commissions galore.

IX

And he dat will not go to mass
Shall be turn out and look like an ass,

X

But now de hereticks all go down,
By Creish and shaint Patrick, de nation's our own.

XI

Dare was an old prophecy found in a bog,
"Ireland shall be ruled by an ass, and a dog."

XII

And now dis prophecy is come to pass,
For Talbot's de dog, and Ja......es is de ass.

83

24814

Cease, O my sad soul

From "New Ayres and Dialogues"

Henry Purcell

so un-kind I may as well com-plain Un - to the wind.

I attempt from Love's sickness to fly

From "The Indian Queen"

Henry Purcell

In moderate time, with expression

p

I at-

p

rit.

tempt from Love's sick-ness to fly_____ in__ vain, Since I am, my-

p

cresc.

f rall.

Fine

self, my own fe - ver, since I am, my - self, my own fe - ver and pain.

cresc.

f rall.

24814

No more now, no more now, fond heart, with pride should we

swell, Thou canst not raise forc-es, thou canst not raise

forc-es e-nough to re-bel! I at-tempt from Love's

sick-ness to fly in vain, Since

I am, my - self, my own fe - ver, since I am, my -

self, my own fe - ver_ and_ pain; For Love has more

pow'r and less mer - cy than Fate To make us_ seek

ru - in, to_ make us seek ru - in, and love those that hate.

D. C. al Fine

When I have often heard

From "The Fairy Queen"

Henry Purcell

Quickly

1. When I have of-ten heard young maids com-plain-ing,
2. Should he em-ploy all his wit in de-ceiv-ing,

That when men prom-ise most they most___ de-ceive,
Stretch his in-ven-tion and art-ful-ly feign,

Then I thought none of them wor-thy my gain-ing,
I find such charms, such true joy in be-liev-ing,

And what they swore I would nev-er be-lieve.
I'll have the plea-sure, let him have the pain.

Dido's Lament

From "Dido and Æneas"

Henry Purcell

laid, — am laid ———— in earth, may my wrongs — cre-

ate no trou-ble, no trouble in thy breast;

Let us dance, let us sing

From "Dioclesian"

Henry Purcell

Let us rev - el, let us rev - el _ and play, let us, let us

rev - el _ and play, And re - joice _

_ whilst we _ may, Since old Time, since old

Time these de - lights _ will re - move.

colla voce

Hence, hence with your trifling deity

From Shadwell's version of
"Timon of Athens"

Bass Song

Henry Purcell

24814

al - ways, al - ways keeps us free

from that blind child - ish pow'r.

Love makes you languish and look pale, And

sneak and sigh, sigh, sigh and whine; But o-ver us no

Arise, ye subterranean winds

Bass Song

From "The Tempest"

Henry Purcell

Quickly

A-rise, a - rise, ye sub - -

ter - ra - nean winds,

winds, More to dis - tract their guilt - y minds!

stacc.

A - rise, ____ ye winds, a - rise, ____ ye

Rise__ and o - bey! Rise__ and o - bey__

the pow'r - - - -

- - - - - -

- ful Prince, the__ pow'r - - ful Prince o' th'air!

rall.

colla voce

Next, Winter comes slowly

Bass Song

From "The Fairy Queen"

Henry Purcell

Be - numb'd with hard frosts   and with snow cov - er'd   o'er, be -

numb'd with hard frosts   and with snow   cov - er'd   o'er,   Prays the

Sun to   re - store him, prays the sun to   re - store him, and   sings

as be - fore.

Shepherd, shepherd, leave decoying

Duet for Two Trebles

From "Orpheus Britannicus"

Henry Purcell

Nymphs and Shepherds

From "The Libertine"

Words by
Thomas Shadwell
(Poet Laureate: 1688-92)

Music by
Henry Purcell
Accompaniment by*
Miles B. Foster

* Purcell only gives a Bass, unfigured, below the voice-part

24814

this, this is Flo - ra's ho - ly - day, this is

Flo - ra's ho - ly - day, this is Flo - ra's ho - ly -

day! Sa - cred to ease

and hap - py love, To

dancing, to mu - - - sic, to danc-ing, to

leggiero

mu - - - - - sic and to po - et-ry.

cresc. *dim.* *r.h.* *p dolce*

mf *dim.*

Your flock may now, now, now, now, now, now, now, now, now, now,

dim.

tranquillo *cresc.*

now, se - cure - ly rove Whilst you ex -

112

press, whilst you ex - press_____ your

jol - li-try! Nymphs and shep-herds,

come a - way, come a - way, Nymphs and shep-herds,

come a - way, come a - way, come, come, come, come a - way!

24814

Phillis, talk not more of passion

Daniel Purcell
(1660 ? - 1740)

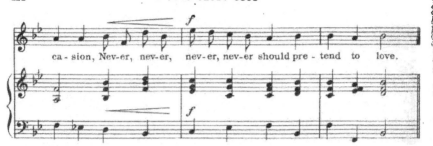

ca - sion, Nev-er, nev-er, nev-er, nev-er should pre - tend to love.

Hon - our, that so＿ oft you＿ men-tion, Love pos - sess - ing

once your mind, A - las, is but a vain＿ pre-

ten - sion Wo - men use, that＿ won't be kind.＿

24814

CPSIA information can be obtained
at www.ICGtesting.com
Printed in the USA
BVOW06*1542141117
500276BV00026B/149/P